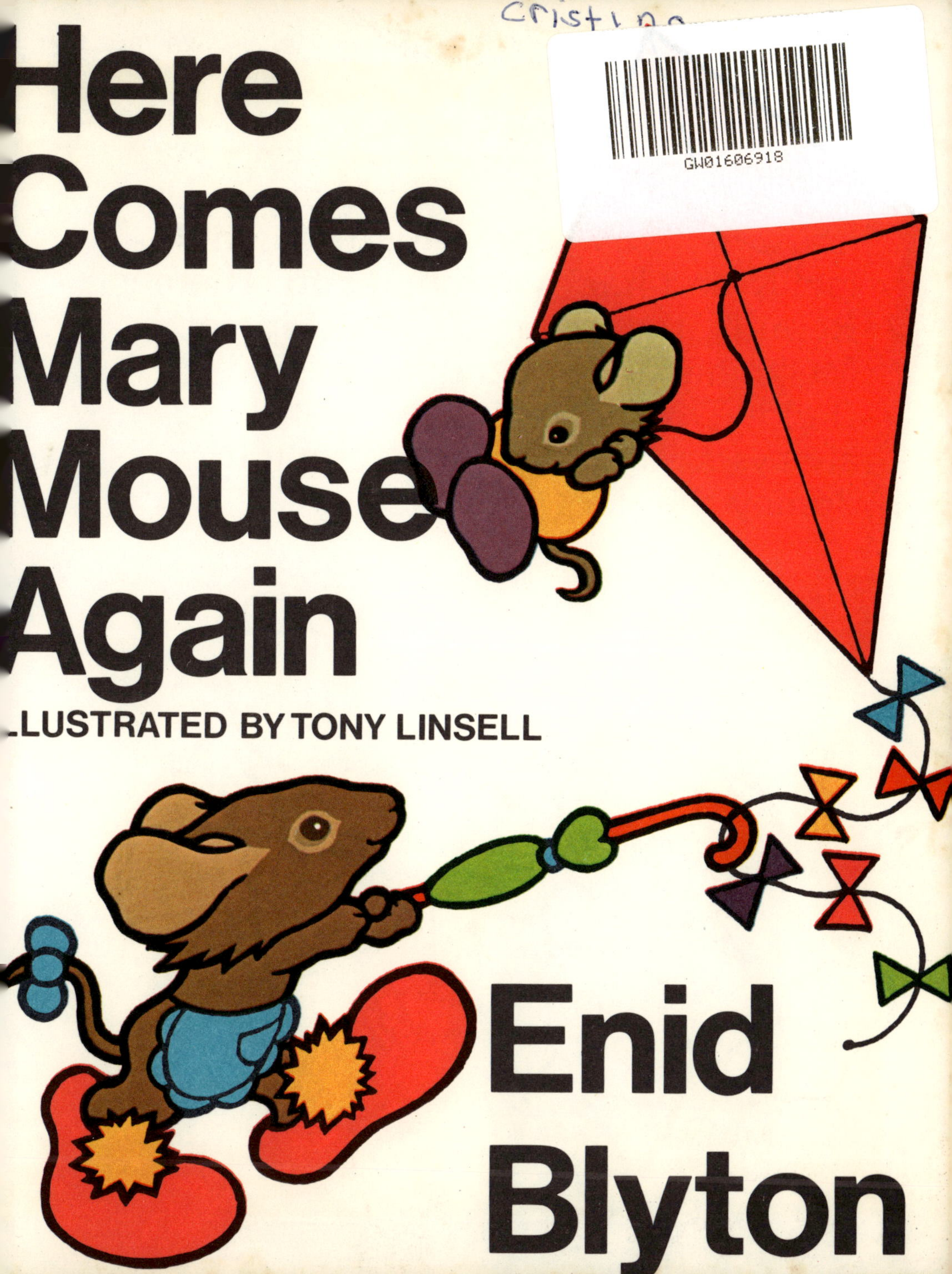

Here Comes Mary Mouse Again

ILLUSTRATED BY TONY LINSELL

Enid Blyton

ROUNDY AND THE SCOOTER

Mary Mouse lives in a little doll's house where she looks after the doll family and her own family too. There is Roundy, the youngest. And Pip and Melia, his brother and sister. And Daddy Doll and Mummy Doll, always smiling. And not forgetting Jumpy the dog, of course.

Whiskers is Mary Mouse's husband. He looks after the garden for Daddy Doll.

Mary Mouse and Whiskers have six children mice, Frisky, Scamper, Squeaker, Woffly, Patter and Tiny, playing in the garden. Squeaker is the naughty mouse.

He has a fine scooter which he lets Roundy play with.

'If Roundy rides your scooter, he must keep in the garden,' said Mary Mouse.

But Roundy is almost as naughty as Squeaker, for when no one is looking he opens the gate and goes out in the street.

He scooted down a hill and frightened a dog and the dog knocked down a cyclist. A big car swerved away from the fallen cyclist and ran into a bus.

And there was almost a disaster as the bus almost knocked down two children. Dear oh dear, the two children were Pip and Melia, coming home from school.

Up came a policeman with a big note-book.

'That car made me run on to the pavement,' said the bus driver.

'I had to swerve because of the fallen cyclist,' said the car-driver.

'I couldn't help falling off because of the dog,' said the cyclist.

'And that little boy on the scooter scared the dog,' said an old lady.

Poor little Roundy!

'You were breaking the speed limit, down that hill,' said the Policeman to Roundy. And he took Pip, Melia and Roundy home.

Roundy was so upset that Pip gave him his best motor-car, because he was sorry for him, and Melia gave him her toy monkey.

SQUEAKER AND THE KITE

The next day Daddy Doll gave Melia and Pip a brand new kite which they went to the park to fly.

They all took turns in holding the string. Then there was trouble, for when Squeaker held the string the kite carried him away. Soon he was just a speck in the sky as Mary Mouse and Mummy Doll watched in horror.

So Pip set off with a satchel full of food, to find the flying Squeaker. He walked and walked until he came to some elm trees.

At the top of the trees were some rook's nests. And from the nests, very faintly, he could hear someone crying 'Help, Help.'

Brave Pip climbed the tree to the top. And there he found Squeaker in the nest. Now what were they to do? How would they ever get down?

Then an enormous rook landed on the nest with a flurry of wings and feathers.

'Please, Mr Rook, would you spread your big wings and carry us home?'

The rook cawed loudly and opened his wings. Pip and Squeaker climbed aboard and the rook flew them home.

TEDDY AND THE MISSING EYE

One morning Teddy the Bear came to visit Mummy Doll, looking very sad.

'My dear Teddy,' said Mummy Doll. 'What ever has happened to your eye?'

'It's gone,' said Teddy.

'How did that happen?' asked Mummy Doll, amazed.

'It came loose and fell down a drain. I couldn't get it out again,' said poor old Teddy, most distressed.

So they went to Mary Mouse to ask her what to do.

'Dear oh me, I shall have to go out into the big world and find another glass eye for Teddy,' said Mary Mouse bravely. For there were all sorts of dangers for tiny mice in the big world. There were big dogs and cats, and people with enormous feet.

After a long walk she found a nursery with a work-basket. And in the basket she found a boot-button eye which nobody wanted.

'Just right for Teddy,' she said.

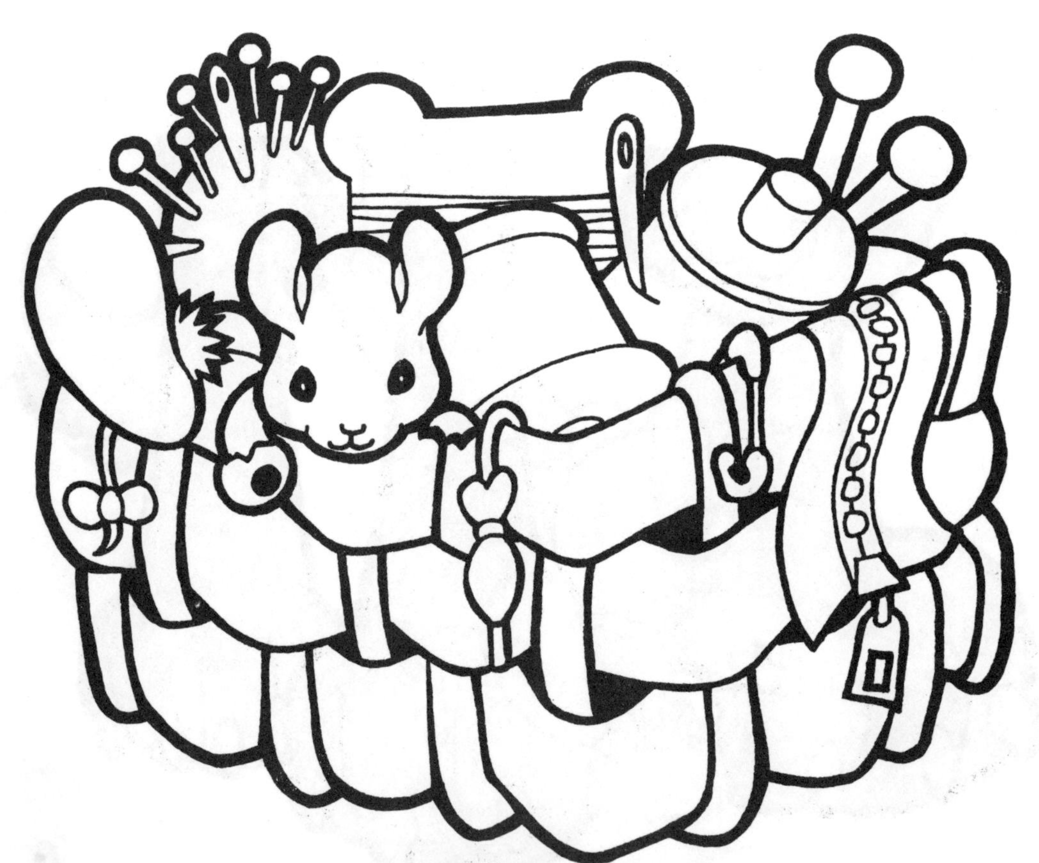

And Mummy Doll sewed it on for Teddy. And all was well again, except that Teddy was a bit cross eyed. But he didn't mind.

JUMPY AND THE DUSTBIN

Now Jumpy the dog was always upsetting dustbins. He made an awful mess for Mary Mouse to clear up. She told him not to, but he always did it again.

One day he climbed right into a dustbin. And just as he was scrabbling about in the mess, Mary Mouse came along. She didn't know he was in the dustbin and stuck the lid on it. Poor old Jumpy was really stuck.

And soon the dustman came along and emptied the rubbish and Jumpy into the dust-cart.

'Woof, woof, woof,' barked the rubbish.

'The rubbish is barking,' cried the dustman in alarm. 'The rubbish has come alive,' he shouted, and rushed off down the road.

Jumpy went home, very quietly. Mary Mouse couldn't understand at all, why Jumpy was so good for the rest of the day.

PIP'S SEVENTH BIRTHDAY

Very soon it was to be Pip's seventh birthday. Seven is a lovely age to be! Mary Mouse and the little mice were all planning surprises for Pip but they didn't tell him.

Mummy and Daddy Doll had bought him a beautiful tricycle, but they didn't say anything either.

Melia had arranged a big party. And Mary Mouse had bought crackers and balloons, but they all kept it a secret.

Poor old Pip thought everyone had forgotten his birthday. He was so sad that he packed a bag to run away on his birthday. But Mummy Doll found it.

'You're not running away on your birthday, Pip, are you?' said Mummy Doll.

And then all the surprises came out. There was a new train from Melia, the tricycle from Daddy Doll, a cake from Mary Mouse and lots of other things. Pip had so many presents and such a party. He was almost buried by it all.

'Oh thank you,' said Pip. 'What a lovely family you are.' And here they all are, all together. What a family Mary Mouse has!